You Deserve All The Credit: A Financial Guide With Proven Steps to Fix Your Credit, Manage Your Spending and Create Income

Attorney Cynthia Young-Shepard

This book was inspired by 3 people (1) God without HIM I would not have had the vision to continue in every realm of my life. Thank HIM for instilling discernment in me. (2) My Mom-Marjorie Baker Young Sanders a.k.a SUPERMOM. She is the most positive powerful classy unbreakable person I know and (3) my ex-husband Attorney Winston Shepard, II who repeated to me for years. "Work Smarter Not Harder". "Make the Money Work For You".

Acknowledgements

Where do I begin with the acknowledgements? First thank God for giving me the strength to complete this project in the midst of a tragedy. Having this unfinished manuscript gathering dust it finally became a priority by Your Grace. The devil sent his warriors dressed in sheeps clothing to destroy me, I used their attack and their shortcomings to uplift myself. Thank you to the Bar Association who provided me this time to finish this book. Thank you to my lovely mom Marjorie Baker Young Sanders. Thank you for being a mom not a sister or a friend, JUST THE BEST MOM IN THE WORLD. Thank you for pushing me when I was exhausted and for encouraging me my whole life. Thank you for letting me be a child when I was a child and reciprocating respect when I became an adult. You are the strongest and best mom I know. You are my Awesome Wonder!!! Finally thank you to my father, Bob Barnes Jr., may he continue to Rest In Heavenly Paradise. Thank you for telling me not to work in a factory. Thank you for telling me never to smoke. I think 50% of my intelligence came from you, thank you for being smart. I thank God for having you in my life for 47 glorious years. It is a true blessing to have both parents and not to have a void, such as that. I know that having my 2 parents is a priceless Gift From God. To know both parents and they know me, not just in pictures, is the biggest blessing of all.

Thank you to my siblings who always believed in me and knew I would get strong again: Jeffrey Lee Young, Richard Alan Young, Crystal Renee Young, Raqea Rachel Stevenson Sanders-Davis and Devion Sanders.

To my friend Charnette Henderson. Thank you for editing this book and always being there in my time of need. To V. Bradley, Jr., continue to Rest in Heaven.

Regarding the sketches in the book. Thank you Attorney S. Hawkins for pointing me to a major resource to create most of the sketches. Even though it took me awhile for me to act and hire someone to bring my vision to paper, I DID IT!

TABLE OF CONTENTS

Acknowledgements 3

Introduction 6

STEP 1- You "Are" Defined By Your Finances But You Can Change Them 11

STEP 2- Create More Money To Obtain Financial Control Faster 20

"Tax Refund Rich". 27

STEP 3 – You Must Open All Mail to Get Organized 30

STEP 4 - Reprioritize Spending Habits: Cut. Save. Pay Old Bills. Save Again 35

STEP 5 – Set Yourself Free 44

STEP 6 - Good Credit vs. Bad Credit 49

BANKRUPTCY INFORMATION SHEET 59

STEP 7 – Last Resort: Bankruptcy 64

CHECKLIST 72

Introduction

We hear about, read about and watch YouTube videos on How to Have A1 Credit and How to Manage Money. Well this book will demonstrate proven steps to get your finances and credit in order. It will show you how to get *"In The Black and out of the Red"*. It shows that to obtain A1 credit and clear up bad debt will not happen if you have no money to do it with.

TRUTH #1 Your Debt Is Overwhelming and Finances Are In The Red. You Need To Get In the Black With Your Finances.

PHRASES IN THE BLACK

"The company's in the black again"

Synonyms

Good credit, available funds, debt-free, out of debt; solvent; financially sound; able to pay one's debts, creditworthy; of good financial standing; solid, secure; profit-making, profitable

That is in the "BLACK"

"When you get in debt you become a slave." -Andrew Jackson

I began my financial responsibility journey at the age of 22, fresh out of undergraduate school. I knew it was no hope for me if I did not first get out of debt. Instead of buying a new car like everyone else with my first job; I got a cash car from my mom, (well free) a grey Chevy Cavalier that leaked and rained inside. This was actually a step above the Renault Alliance, which I happily gave away.

My first job out of college was at the Saginaw Housing Commission. They loaned me a car to use while at work, so I did not have to worry about the rain except on the weekends. I drove my vehicle, (whose passenger

door did not open either), for 2 years and within that time frame I became completely debt free. I bought my first new car at a 0% interest rate. Shortly thereafter, I had my first property built from the ground up at the age of 24. LIFE was good. Not bad for a girl from Daniel Heights Housing Projects, who chose education and good credit over being a drug mule☺. (It was the 90's; some not so smart ladies were doing it. I was smarter than that; broke but smarter).

After 15 years on "Easy Street" and with "Hard Work", 1 failed marriage, debt overwhelmed me; once again I was able to rebuild my credit. This goes to show that at any age or stage good credit can be accomplished more than once. The elusive 700 credit score is real and obtainable. My first step always is to do an assessment of my finances and prepare a roadmap to get out of debt, AGAIN. At this point I knew I was

"Roberta in the Red". I knew I had to work harder and smarter to get in the financially stable Black Zone. I use the alias, Roberta, sometimes to refer to myself so I did not feel connected to the debt. You know like when you answer the phone and it is a bill collector, they ask for you and you say she not here. Well that was me I was Roberta and Cynthia was not available. Sadly this avoidance of debt does not work and is not progressive so I changed.

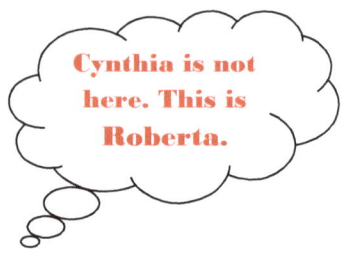

THE DISGUSTED LOOK WHEN ALL YOUR FINANCES ARE IN THE RED

STEP 1- You "Are" Defined By Your Finances But You Can Change Them

They are personal to you. Where you want to go with your finances is up to you. Start by examining where you are currently. This is the hard part but you must look at your finances no matter how bad they are. Assuming you are working a job or self employed, look at your pay check honestly.

Your available spendable income is your NET it isn't around $1,400.00 bi-weekly it is $1,292.00. You only have $1,292.00 to budget if you figure $1,400.00 you are starting off in the negative already.

False reality will create negative financial results. You want honest positive everything by the end of this BOOK. In order for you to live in your truth and reach your goal easier and faster; you must live in your truth.

The first thing that you should do when you receive your pay check, if not before is to make a budget. Meaning every pay check write down how you spend every dime of your pay check. Start off by paying yourself, and that is not with a pair of Giuseppe Zanotti; *Cartiers* or Pure White Hennessy; by putting 10% in your emergency fund account. Previously, every book you read said put it into your savings account, but it is better to put in Emergency Fund and only spend for Emergency.

NOTE: Savings Account is where you save money for a long term reason or just for retirement. Emergency Fund is for car repairs or medical expenses.

7 QUICK WAYS TO CREATE BETTER SPENDING HABITS

(1) Create A Plan.

Prioritize your spending based on what is important. Determine your goal. If it is getting out of debt, list debt at top budget sheet (after food, shelter, utilities and transportation). (Use Enclosed Budget Sheet or App on your phone).

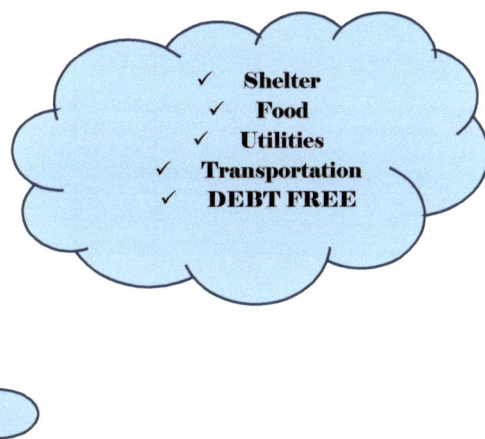

You need a concrete plan. Everyone cannot live with their parents for free, so the top priority is shelter-rent or mortgage. If you rent or obtain a mortgage you need downsize. Your new place just needs to be SMALL, SAFE and CLEAN. Or consider getting a roommate temporarily. For example: a niece who can only pay $300.00 a month plus food, while she's in college.

WRITE IT OUT AND KNOW WHAT MONEY YOU HAVE

BUDGET SHEET

INCOME	MONTH	Aug	Sept	Oct	Nov	Dec
Wages						
Taxes						
Miscellaneous Deductions						
TOTALS/NET						
EXPENSES						
Mortgage/Rent						
Utilities						
Cell Phone						
Home Repairs						
Home Security/ADT						
TOTALS						
DAILY LIVING						
Groceries						
Child Care						

Dry Cleaning					
Dining Out					
Daily Living Totals					
TRANSPORTATION					
Gas/fuel					
Insurance					
Repairs					
Parking/Public Transportation					
Car Note					
TOTALS					

(2) Research.

If you must buy something, research it before you shop. With the internet at your fingertips, you can make the best informed decision. If you are in the market to buy a big-ticket item such as a TV, researching can help you compare prices.

(3) Avoid Your Spending Triggers, We All Have Them!

We shop when we are depressed, usually about money, which makes the situation worse. Pause a day and then see if you still want to spend *that* money *that* you do not have. It will not seem that appealing in 24 hours. If you fall short and make a purchase, just return it the next day with the receipt and get your money back.

(4) Find An Accountability Partner.

Just like we do when we are dieting, the same concept except we are dieting from SPENDING. For married couples, that would be your husband or wife. For singles accountability, partner would be a trusted family member or a responsible friend. Discuss your big money goals with this person. Then check in with them before making big purchases. The teamwork factor is super important!

(5) Do Not Shop While You Wait.

A 2012 Google study found that 28% of people who use their mobile device to shop do so while waiting in line. I AM GUILTY OF THIS TOO. It is tempting to browse *Amazon*, *Ann Taylor* or *FashionNova* while you are sitting in the car pool line at school, or in the waiting room at the doctor's office. If you know you will be waiting in line, keep a book or magazine in your car to help past the time.

(6) Develop Patience.

When dealing with money you have to have the WINNING mentality because the road requires patience and can get rough. Know that your finances are tailored made to you! Buying in the midst of excitement a.k.a the fever can lead to a real financial headache. Instead take your time; 24 hours should do the trick. Do not worry it, will be there tomorrow. You will typically wake up the next day with little less excitement over the item, which can help you make a more rational buying decision.

(7) Look For Savings Before You Buy.

If you regularly shop at a certain store, then you probably know the times they have their best deals. Check out your supermarkets sales circular so you can stock up on the on-sale items you love. Keep an eye on your favourite clothing store so you can buy the out-of-season coats, shirts and shorts on clearance. Sign up for store email updates and check online for coupons before you purchase. A little work ahead of time goes a long way. It will save you a bit of money now, but a ton in the long run! https://www.everydollar.com/blog/create-better-spending-habits

This goes back to my original principal: Look at the net amount of money you really have to spend, devise a plan and stick to it. If insufficient income is the issue, then you cannot have an emergency fund right now. Which also means you should not be spending a nickel outside of the necessities.

SOLUTION: Obtain a second income, Plain & Simple. You cannot get off work and watch HULU, NETFLIX and XBOX, SOULJA Boy Console or PS4 anymore; you have to work a second job.

MY CREDIT SMART NOTES #1

TRUTH #2 Make Peace With Your Money. You Need & Want It.

"The Way To Wealth Depends On Two Things Industry and Frugality" - Benjamin Franklin

Do not spend money as fast as you get it. If your payday is Friday wait until Saturday to pay or schedule a bill payment. Generally if a person is paid on Friday, by Monday, 85% of the pay check is gone. Part of this is panic, impulse shopping, or rewarding yourself. If you wait at least 24 hours to spend any of the money your decisions will be more rational. More than likely you will buy what you need and not what you want.

I work so I am buying kids and me something. I will pay bills later.

STEP 2- Create More Money To Obtain Financial Control Faster

Create more money because you need it☺. Many do not believe that there is cash in your old clothes and other items. Look up all the consignment shoppes in your area. Check the Better Business Bureau website to be sure there are no complaints for them not paying consignees. This is a great place for you to sell used items like shoes, etc.

Check out these websites:

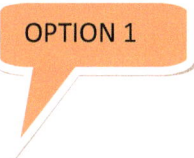

www.lovemetwotimesshop.com

www.runwayfashionexchange.com

www.narts.com

www.alexissuitcase.com

www.poshmark.com

The most "high-traffic" place to sell things is on the internet. Start with *EBay* or Amazon they have a good reputation. *EBay* has over 10.3 million listings in the clothes category. The reason is no other place that makes it easy to search for brand names like Juicy

Couture, Coach, Gucci and Ralph Lauren (which are best sellers). Another positive is that shipping can be covered by the buyer, commissions and fees are minimal. Make sure that when you are listing an item; take a well lit picture even if it is with your camera phone. The goal is to sell the item and put a few bucks in your pocket. I started out by putting my mom antiques for sale on *EBay*. I cashed in and paid some bills.

A former co-worker, Heather Murdoch, created more income, from sales on *EBay*, where she sells exclusively on *EBay*. She updates her post and marketing efforts every day after work. It started out as a hobby to help her forget that she was at a crappy job. Then she started making money, paying bills and kept making more money. Subsequently her finances were in the BLACK, and she now works her *EBay* business ¾ of the time a great part time gig. Good job Heather!

OPTION 2

You can also try www.craigslist.com. It has gotten some bad press, so be careful. If you have a business or work in an office, consider scheduling pickups at office during business hours. Take at least 3 pictures to put on the website. Do not waste a bunch of time trying to describe the item to potential buyers via email.

MY STORY...

After an unsuccessful marriage I sold my wedding dress online for $1200, after buying it off season on sale for $500. Although the marriage failed, that dress helped get my debt into the BLACK. I paid one bill in full with that money. Everything helps and you cannot stop chopping away at the debt.

Minimally you can create $350.00 a month from re-selling your old stuff. Keep that money to create an emergency fund for car repairs, settle old debts or pay off house or car early. Setup a separate account with your Credit Union just for this fund. Examples of good credit unions are ones associated with your college or the military.

OPTION 3

There is no shame in honest work. You cannot sit and wait for things to happen. If Cosby Show actor Geoffrey Owens after making millions can work at Trader Joes; you can definitely rideshare with Lyft or Uber to make more money.

Lyft car service has advertisements right now begging for drivers. Stop talking yourself out of opportunities and do something to get out of the RED and into the BLACK. Increase your income-LEVEL UP YOUR LIFE.

What is Lyft? It is a taxi or private car. It is more commonly referred to as a rideshare that you communicate with from your mobile phone using the Lyft Driver App, to accept ride requests.

Lyft connects you to a passenger within minutes. The average driver is paid $30.00 per ride. You have the option to get paid daily and/or weekly. Just think, if you work weekends for 10 rides for a year. That would be $300.00 a week, which is $15,600.00 a year, $1,200 a month by working part time. That could put a big dent in private school tuition or reducing the amount of old bills. I support and endorse Lyft because I used this as second income to get on top of my finances part-time. Here is the link to sign up:

www.lyft.com/drivers/cynthia375005.com

https://partners.uber.com/i/cynthias13073ue

Another idea is to join an established online business with an established Brand of followers. Naurice, another former co-worker, joined a business to supplement her low pay and created an additional $600 per month by selling jewellery online. Subsequently she built her business to the point where she only has to work a JOB part time.

http://paparazziaccessories.com/128526

Cosmetic company Mary Kay Cosmetics, Inc. is still a flourishing company and was the sixth largest network marketing company in the world in 2015, with a wholesale volume of US $3.7 billion. The company was founded by Mary Kay Ash in 1963. Research how to become a representative. They give out pink Cadillacs, of course you have to earn them. Go to this representative website. She has worked for Mary Kay for over 20 years, earned many awards and is very helpful.

www.marykay.com/tmallen

After over a decade of working as a successful Real Estate Agent and Nail Technician. Crystal realized she needed additional income.

She found a little easy gig that no one in this world would have told her about, but by networking, this position was found. Both of us worked as drivers

delivering prescription medicines and other emergency equipment (legal of course). It was a 24/7 business, which allows you to work day or night shifts you pick your schedule. Average income for part time drivers was about $500.00 weekly, and that is just working 8 hours for 3 days, in your spare time. That is $2,000.00 a month or $24,000.00 a year.

With some of these options, if you are in a real serious financial crisis you can just work straight through for a few days and get the cash to manage the emergency. These are non-traditional jobs, but get the financial crisis handled and the monies rolling with some effort. It was one of the easiest jobs I have ever had in my life, shot out to Leigh Smith of Priority Dispatch, thanks for the opportunity and research material.☺

My only complaint, where in the hell were these jobs when I was struggling in college? I could have racked up tons of money while delivering medication and listening to my college courses in my vehicle.

ACT. BELIEVE. RECEIVE.

You have to create NOW money and not wait for a yearly raise from a job. By the time you get a raise the interest on bill will have eaten up the raise.

If you are a **Tax Refund Rich Person**, stop that habit this upcoming year. Lets address that tax refund that a lot of people receive a.k.a.

"Tax Refund Rich"

- Do not buy a car, that will only last until your next refund next year.

- Make sure to go ahead and pay back that person who you borrowed money from based on tax refund.

- Do not go out and buy things you cannot maintain, like the latest biggest smart phone and you are not running a business from it.

- Do not run to all the fancy restaurants, you will just keep making them rich. Benihana, J. Alexander and Reb Lobster owners are already rich and with good credit.

- Do not go out and get surgery unless it is an investment in your occupation. (Just to look good at next cook out is not an occupation). A BBL is not a necessity enough to use your tax refund on.

- Do not jump up and pay for a cruise or, a trip of any kind because by the time the cruise comes you will be out of tax money and struggling because you did not invest in correcting your financial situation. Instead of lavish purchases fix your credit and financial status.

- Do not take money from your kids to buy your boyfriend a gun to protect the family, when not 1 kid is his. Tell him to fight the burglar you are paying off your debt to make a better life for all of you.

***Get your credit together so you can get a reliable vehicle for longer period of time. The idea of being Tax Refund Rich should be changed to Get My Credit Right Rich! For more information visit this website. www.creditbeastinc.om

MY CREDIT SMART NOTES #2

TRUTH #3 These are YOUR bills. You Created Them, Now Lets Crush Them.

"For Every Minute Spent In Organizing An Hour Of Your Life Is Earned" -Benjamin Franklin

It hurt me to my soul to actually go through and organize my mail. I had an office box, post office box and two home addresses.

Mail was everywhere, I discovered that some bills I paid in advance, some over paid and some were not paid at all. I went to the clearance section of Office Depot and

bought whatever files they had and organized my bills by:

- Office vs. Home
- Year
- Collection Status
- Paid in full
- Pay off within 90 days.

It was a relief and a form of freedom that cannot be described. I WAS THEN FULLY AWARE OF MY DEBT.

You can do the same thing. Go to Dollar Tree, *TJMaxx*, or 5 Below they have tons of organization tools and setup a station/box just to organize your bills.

STEP 3 – You Must Open All Mail to Get Organized

Sometimes bills don't get paid because you lack a system, or sometimes anxiety about finances creates a state of denial like if I don't open them, they are not there. But that only compounds the damage. We have handled the organizational part, now lets get to work. So take a RED BULL (or alcoholic drink of choice), grab those envelopes or click that mouse and take these steps to regain control.

A. Sort your bills. Make bins or folders labelled "pay now," "pay next week," pay next month" and "paid". Print all of them out; yes even the *ebills*. Store them in a central location like a china cabinet, where you can see them. You need to see your bills to inspire you, to see your goal or purpose for working. When new bills come in the mail, open and file them immediately. Experts say remove from dining room table because you will never properly digest your food looking at bills. I have experienced this and it is true, however if you do not see them you might not pay them. So take the good with the bad. It is important to see them.

B. Mark your calendar. After sorting your bills, write the send-by dates (so they will arrive by the due date) on a calendar. By paying on time you avoid interest, penalties and late fees, which average about $35. Find the calendar app on your phone that works for you and add notifications for each payment date that will alarm 1-2 days before each pay day.

C. Make a weekly appointment with your bills. Set aside 30 minutes to 1 hour each week to pay and review bills. Empty the "pay now" folder, and rotate the bills from the "pay next week" folder to "pay now." Move some of the "pay next month" bills to the "pay next week" folder. Be sure to update your calendar with new send-by dates.

D. Save your old bills. Put paid bills into the "paid" folder. Store two to three months worth just in case there is a question of what amount was paid. As you add bills to the folder purge and shred the oldest ones. Clear your mind and house of this worry.

E. AUTO PAY. NO WAY. Although signing up for your bank's online automatic-bill payment feature to avoid risk of late fees is a good concept; you are low on money and 1 overdraft fee could worsen the situation and spiral your finances out of control. You may end up spending more money on overdraft fees than the bill. Use the old method of purchasing money orders and crossing them off your checklist of bills. You would be amazed at how many people file bankruptcy having 2% of the debt being overdraft fees. In an ideal situation we would use auto-pay, but not right now catch up on bills and do not risk wasting money on bank fees. (Sorry Wells Fargo and Huntington Bank). The "money order and envelope system" still works and is effective. A better and more modern form of payment is PayPal or Cash App; use this to pay back friends or vendors, like a Lawn Care Service, you may owe.

Close those unused bank accounts. If you are with a credit union stay with that banking institution. Otherwise, just one major bank account is needed. So what if they gave you a new book bag or $250 as a sign up fee. Close the account! Remember you have no money for overdraft fees, or monthly fees, just so you can have multiple accounts. CLOSE IT, until you can clear up some debt.

MY CREDIT SMART NOTES #3

TRUTH #4 Budgeting - Does Not Mean That You Are Poor It Means You Do Not Want To Be Poor.

"A Budget is Telling Your Money Where to Go, Instead of Wondering Where it Went" – John C. Maxwell

Quick **tips**:

- Take your lunch to work.
- Shop around for cheap gas.
- Use rewards cards.

I saved over $3000.00 a year taking my lunch more often and using rewards cards for gas.

It was hard developing this habit, but after looking at my bank statements and seeing my $500 a month going to restaurants, making them richer. I had to cut that out.

Review your bank statement as soon as you get it. First for errors and second to see where your money is going. You should say, "No more: That you do not know where your money is going." You will because it will be in black and white. Do not stick your head in the sand. Identify the wrong trail, then stop the track you are on and redirect yourself.

STEP 4 - Reprioritize Spending Habits: <u>Cut</u>. <u>Save</u>. <u>Pay Old Bills</u>. <u>Save Again</u>

Stay Positive. Nothing is more inspiring than learning from your mistakes. You have to deal with the reality this shortfall. Some of the tricks of creating more and eliminating short falls is to bundle your internet, phone and cable bills. Most companies give you a break when you bundle and then give more of a break when you renew your contract (you have the advantage at the beginning of the contract and at renewal time).

On the other hand having the bills separated is good just in case there is an emergency and your monies are needed for other bills/things. If you need to you can turn off the cable and you can still use a friends password for Netflix or Amazon Prime, but without the internet and you will not totally be cut off from the WORLD. You can keep minimum cable and use internet at library or *Tim Hortons*. It is more cumbersome without no cable, no internet and no house phone. If you got kids they are going to worry the heck out of you so it is worth having them separate just in case money is short.

When you begin reprioritizing your spending habits talk to the kids. Let them know that there are some financial constraints and things are going to have to change with some of the services in the house. Maybe no more purchasing of games, now you rent or buy re-used PSP games and rent Xbox games or swap between friends. The bottom-line is that the excessive spending habits must stop. End the fast food restaurant visits for the kids too. Pull out the biggest bill like the light bill and review it with them. If they just understand a part of what you are saying hopefully they will understand to turn the lights out in rooms not occupied. Do not let them walk around with their heads in the sand while the adults stress and scream.

Also limit your daily Latte to once a week and bike it to work, especially during warm months to save money. This does not mean that you have to stop living, just watch your money output until you get a grip on it.

Extreme Couponing, shown on the TLC network is a show about people who use couponing in their daily lives so much that they are getting items for free and sometimes retailers are giving them money back. I

could not adapt to the extreme mentality, but did incorporate couponing into my life; It just makes sense. For example: Between *Arby's,* KFC and *Wendy's,* why pay for 2 of anything when you can pay for 1 and get second one free with a coupon. You can feed yourself and your kid in the back seat, or just save it for later.

There are web sites, magazine articles, TV news stories, and newspaper articles on making a plan to save. Many people overlook this huge opportunity to save. Always keep your eyes open to all savings. Billions of coupons are circulating in the U.S. everyday. Sunday newspapers and online coupons make it so easy. They really do work, it can be time consuming but you can get the kids involved. Form a friend group couponing. Exchange similar coupons for products or share coupons for other items that compliment the needs of all.

Up to 90 percent of coupons are in the Sunday

newspaper along with the valuable sales inserts and circulars. In some areas of the United States the Sunday papers are sold at Dollar Tree. You can buy 2 newspapers for 1 and have double coupons.

Also at Dollar Tree there is a 50% off the $1.00 section. These items are usually in a basket at end of the register. I always get the dishwashing liquid and cleaning supplies from 50 cent basket. Items are usually open or slightly used. For example: 1/3 of washing liquid gone. That is fine the 2/3's remaining is only 50 cent.

Styles come, and styles go. Some come around again and again. When it comes to saving money, clipping coupons is still in style. You can find a coupon for nearly everything you buy.

Spending options multiply with coupons

The number of coupons redeemed did not fall last year for the first time since coupons usage began to decline in the 90s. Metro area grocery stores are receiving more coupons than ever!

Money saved by using coupons has a multitude of uses. It can be used to pick up other things, to payoff old bills, build up savings, or get necessities at the drugstore. With all the new ways to save money today – i.e. customer discount cards – coupons can offer an even bigger savings to you.

Remember to be flexible when using coupons:

- ✓ Shop weekly to take advantage of weekly sales
- ✓ Be brand flexible and store flexible
- ✓ Buy two to three copies of the Sunday paper for multiple coupons
- ✓ Look for double coupon deals
- ✓ Print free coupons from the Internet
- ✓ Stock up when your usual items are on sale
- ✓ Combine coupons with discount cards other savings programs and offers
- ✓ Check if the store honours competitor coupons (Wal-Mart does)

Save even more money by keeping a record of the prices of everything on your usual shopping list. Organize it into categories and classify the items as needed. Keep this record with you and search out even more affordable prices at other stores. You can often find your favourite products for a cheaper price. This information, supplemented by coupons, will put more money in your pocket for your emergency fund, or to pay off debt so you can be DEBT FREE.

Organizing is Maximizing Savings

Clean out your junk drawer, instead use it to organize your coupons, do not spend money on buying an official organizer. I saw on *Extreme Couponing* a savvy college student mastered this process. His name was Dominique. He and his fraternity brother used their stock pile of coupon purchases of gelatine to pay for a college pool party. It was awesome and free! On another episode, another college student in Missouri saved $300 a month reducing his grocery bill using coupons. He used that savings to pay on bills or buy books.

We all know that using coupons is beneficial to our wallets, but it is sometimes hard to remember to use them! First, get a mobile coupon organizer and never leave the house without it (keep it sitting on your back seat). Secondly, organize the coupons in the order you shop at the store, i.e., produce first, then meat, dairy, and finally bread, etc.

Once an organizational system is established, then it is easier to quickly pull the coupons needed on the next shopping run. Whether you are shopping for a couple of items, specific ingredients for a favourite dinner, or for a restocking, a well-organized shopper can save 30-80 percent. (www.grocerycouponguide.com)

You can find coupons at lot of great web sites. Visit sites such as:

www.Shoplocal.com

www.Coolsavings.com

www.Couponcabin.com

www.hotcoupons.com

www.Coupons.com

Testimony of Coupon Practices

Dear Cynthia,

I am having a real problem. My husband of 5 years is throwing away money every week by not clipping coupons from the newspaper! I have begged and pleaded but he simply cannot see the savings. With an average savings value of almost $100 every week, clipping coupons is the easiest way to save money on the things we buy every week! How can I get him to put down the computer or XBOX?

Desperate to Save in Dallas

Dear Desperate Dallas,

You have a firm grasp of the simple economics of coupons. Now it is time to demonstrate your savings to your husband so he can see the light. Make it a competition: Each of you browse the computer for coupons and print those you want to use every week. Then both of you go to the store, do the shopping and both of you save big! It's a win win situation! Saving money on the little things adds up to big savings every week. Plus now hubby is involved and did not have to put down his computer.

Attorney Young

MY CREDIT SMART NOTES #4

TRUTH #5 This Is Not Easy But If You Want It Bad Enough You Must Put In The Work.

"To achieve what 1% of the worlds population has (Financial Freedom), you must be willing to do what only 1% dare to do, hard work and perseverance of highest order." – **Manoj Arora, From the Rat Race to Financial Freedom**

Pension and Social Security funds are no longer enough income to live off of. According to the Social Security Administration, the average retirement income as of January 2017 was $1,342.00. Average housing expenses are $800.00, leaving little to nothing for food and gas! So the plan is to create more income even while you are retired.

Between 2015 and 2016, US median household income rose 3.2%, from $57,230 to $59,039, according to a new report released by the U.S. Census Bureau - *September 12, 2017.*

To my knowledge the average inner city income is around $2500 a month or less for the twenty-something's. We must get off this Struggle Bus.

The wealthy have over 7 streams on income lets start by properly utilizing our 1 income plus 6 additional incomes and savings. It is never too late to have more money.

STEP 5 – Set Yourself Free

Today there is a ton of work from home jobs full and part time. Try Kelly Connect, where you work from home when it fits your schedule. Apple Computers and Progressive Insurance are legitimate branded work from home businesses.

Another solution is a low investment business that you own. Of course we all know that there are millions of businesses that you can start, and work from home. For example: A tax business, you pass a 6 week course and you are in business. Do not forget to get a certified verified mentor. There are also franchise options for different businesses like: dry cleaners, coffee shops, insurance agencies, small restaurants, dollar stores and janitorial services, etc. Do not be deceived; although you have support with the franchise, it is still really hard work. So be ready to initially put in what only 1% of people dare to do.

6-TOP FRANCHISE OPPORTUNITIES

- Dream Vacations (Travel & Hospitality) Cash Required $9800 Initial Investment: $3245. You can also find this service where you can work from home with smaller investment for example $300.00. You can work this business and obtain your trip for free. Some states do not even require any type of licensing for this occupation and it is easy to work this along with your primary income until you build this business.

- Cruise Planners, An American Express Travel Representative (Travel & Hospitality) Cash Required $10495 Initial Investment $10,495.

- TSS Photography (Child Services) Cash Required $10,5000 Initial Investment $20,400. Start this business from home first with a good camera for an investment of $800 or less, build your clientele before you join the franchise.

- Payroll Vault (Financial & Tax) Cash Required $35,750 Initial Investment $21,000. This business can begin from home as a tax preparer and then once you build your clientele join the franchise. Software for this start up can start as low as $99.00.

- Professional Janitorial Services (Service) Cash Required $1,500 Initial Investment $5,000. (Look at getting a big contract the requirements but start with a medium contract if possible, like a small office building and then work your way to a government or business contract. GET A MENTOR. Have someone help around the hurdles.

- Amazing Athletes (Child Services) Cash Required $17,500 Initial Investment $25,000. Maybe start a smaller service out of your home before you a join a franchise, that way you are brining clientele to this big investment project.

- Image One (Dry Cleaning & Maintenance) Cash Required $15,000 Initial Investment $29,750. With this franchise option consider having partners. This is good for a husband and wife team.

If you wanted to start a hair business and needed a vendor list for hair, lashes and all your beauty needs contact 24karatkollectionllc@gmail.com. They even have an *ebook* you can download in be in business with minimum start up cost. The company will not leave you alone they are always there for support.

Remember: It does not take money alone to make money; it also takes knowledge and motivation! So get motivated find a business you think you would enjoy doing. You will need a mentor and hit the ground running.

MY CREDIT SMART NOTES #5

TRUTH #6 Quit Spending What You Really Do Not Have.

"The man who never has money enough to pay his debts has too much of something else"-James Basford

The most commonly used credit scoring system, called FICO, rates people from a very risky 300 to a pristine 850. Right now this society is in the middle of a credit score crunch: You need a 700 or better today to have the same treatment you got with a 620 two years ago. Learn your score, you have three FICO scores based on your credit report at the three credit bureaus: Experian, Equifax and Transunion. You can get a free credit report from freecreditreport.com (you can even use your pre-paid credit card), but cancel service within 30 days because you cannot afford any monthly charges.

Client Letter...

Dear Attorney Cynthia,

I was recently released from a State facility after 10 years and my credit score is 397. For the most part these debts happened while I was incarcerated and accounts are in different states. What do I do?

Signed,

Ms. Free Again

Dear Ms. Free Again,

Well congratulations on your freedom. Lets talk about your financial freedom.

#1 Update your contact information on your credit report beginning with names and addresses. #2 If you have any federal debt get those updated and current ASAP. They will accept payments as little as $5.00 a month. #3 Settle and delete collection accounts. Do not waste time arguing about the debt that is actually yours.

These 3 things alone should increase your score dramatically. It does not matter if you are in East Lansing, Michigan or Kingsport, Tennessee the results will be the same. You have the best alibi THE GOVERNMENT.

This is how to settle credit card debt with collection agency.

1. Let's say you owe $15,000 in credit card debt. You negotiate to pay back 50%f of that. You say 50% and they counter with pay 80%, then you settle at 60% that is still a $6000 savings on a debt that you did owe.

2. Your monthly payments. Negotiate a lower monthly payment on everything until you get a handle on your bills and double up payments every time you can.

3. Your account's standing: This is the part that affects your credit score. Request that they change your

account to good standing or to delete the account completely.

*Each state has a law referred to as a "statute of limitations," which spells out the time period during which creditors or collectors may sue borrowers to collect debts. In most states, they run between **4-6 years** after the last payment was made on the debt. So if your debt is at the 5 year mark and you not in a hurry, wait 12 months and it will be stale and uncollectable. At that 6 month mark write letter requesting that this item is deleted because it is now stale because the Statute of Limitations has run out.*

4. Deny all bills that do not belong to you and attach proof of incarceration with your demand to have debt removed from your report. How can some of those cable or light bills be yours and you were living with/on the STATE? Just dig into it.

Again welcome back! Let that STATECATION be your 1 and done.

Attorney Cynthia

STEP 6 - Good Credit vs. Bad Credit

There are three C's of credit: credit cards, charge cards and cash cards. WE are only using cash to get things paid and build up your credit!! The Cash System works. The system is all about taking budgeting back to pure cash. This helps you save money by having the money physically in front of you as you pay for items. The theory is that you will be more likely not to overspend, because you are handing over real cash and not just swiping a card.

Get Smart About Your Credit!

Credit means the right granted to a customer to: (a) defer payment of debt (b) incur debt and defer its payment or (c) purchase property or services and defer payment for the same.

Credit cards are not to be used while you try to become financially free. Credit cards are instruments created by the powers that be to keep you deep in debt. At some point it will keep you awake at night worried about how to pay them. This is time you should be sleeping. By definition credit cards allow you to borrow money from your bank to make purchases, whether buying a Burger or a round trip ticket to ARUBA.

As long as you pay back the money you borrowed within the "grace period" of 25-30 days, you don't have to pay interest on the card.

You now realize the tight budget you are on to pay for living, savings and emergency funds. Do not borrow from any entity or anyone. You say but I got 25-30 days to pay back. Unless you created more money over and above your paycheck; you will not have the money to pay back in 25-30 days. What happens is you will have to pay interest, which is money you owe to the bank-on top of what you borrowed. Now you are digging a deeper hole for yourself. This is similar to the payday loans with 20% interest, you borrowing but do not have the income in the first place to pay back.

Credit Cards are a big NO NO, right now! If you do not listen to this advice and do get a credit card you can only use for emergencies. Emergencies are kidney transplants. Emergencies are not getting a child transported to school across town where they should not be attending any way. The city bus is for that. Quit making up excuses to be financially irresponsible, this causes you to remain in the RED. The ultimate goal is to live in the BLACK with plenty of Greenbacks at your disposal.

Credit cards and charge cards are not the same. There were a few times in my life where the distinction became clearer. I did not actually know this until I worked for Compuware Corporation based in Dallas, Texas. As part of my job they issued me an American Express to use for team expenses. At 24, I could hear my mothers and fathers voice in my head instructing me to always do the right thing, and pay my bills. A college friend, Tracy Charley-Purnell said to me after knowing her for 2 days' "never get a credit card until you have a real job because it would destroy your life". I had only known her for 2 days, but she saw me opening my mail which was full of credit card offers.

I had no reason to believe she was lying or insane and besides she was an upper class man, so I listened and boy was she RIGHT!

A Charge card is a card that requires payment in full every month. It does not have a preset limit, rather purchases get approved based on spending and payment history, financial resources, and credit record. Whereas credit cards have a credit limit and permit users to carry a balance at a specific interest rate. For example, Diners Club was the very first charge card issued and American Express was the second charge card. Both cards were designed to be paid in full each month.

In my case my American Express was based on Compuware Corporation payment history, financial resources and credit report, which was excellent.

Smartly because of the advice of my parents and Tracy Charley- Purnell, I did not use it for personal use. The card was entrusted to me by my employer, but it took me being responsible. I did the right thing and only used charge card for bare minimum job activities.

A cash card will only allow you to make automatic teller machine withdrawals. You use the phone or internet to pay for goods or services in person or over the phone or over the internet. In my case I obtained a bank account to introduce my sister to the financial world. It only allowed cash withdrawals from ATM machine no other transactions was allowed. This prevented unapproved transactions, "I did not know moments", and overdrafts. It worked like a charm until she could fly on her own. The card allows the person to learn discipline, patience and control over spending only what you have. This is my second method of how to spend money. My first choice is CASH! Greenbacks, *Dinero*, *fric*, cheddar, Benjamins, Dead Presidents, coins (in my Kandi Burress voice).

Pay as you go with cash because when you are trying to gain or maintain absolute control of your finances, you must live in the REAL: Real time, real money, not promises for the future or hopes and dreams of the ability to pay. You either have it or you do not. This eliminates future stress in your mind and body. When you pay cash that ends your responsibility. You go off and enjoy the fruits of your cash ability. With your finances live in the NOW and stay in the BLACK! It does not make sense to eat a burger today and pay for it 30 days from now. I have had people come to my office who are oblivious to the fact the energy company reports to the credit bureau. That is why they ask for your social security number to start energy services. After you correct any errors on your credit reports, then boost your score by paying bills on time; reduce credit balances to less than 20% of your limits.

To get top rates today may also require a bigger down payment-20% for a house, 10% for a car having good credit could eliminate a high deposit. And you must show that you have steady income and in the BLACK. Here are the factors that determine credit score:

(1) 30% Low credit card balances

(2) 35% Payment History

(3) 15% Income & credit history

(4) 10% Types of Credit

(5) 10% New Credit

No matter what your yearly income you can accomplish good credit, I did!

The first step is to check for errors and immediately dispute anything that looks unfamiliar. The credit report agency has 30 days to prove debt; if not then it is deleted. Secondly fix addresses and names from your present and past if there are errors. Lastly, make it a hobby to monitor your credit report. Verify all balances on accounts monthly. Before you pay off old debt while you in this process ask the creditor to delete the debt from report in exchange for paying debt. Accept settlement in full only if that strategy does not work. Just paying a little over payments due will help your score as well. Eventually the balance will be 0. Do not avoid paying a bill just because you do not have all the money, pay a partial payment. **Tip**: if you make 2 payments in same month before due date it will increase your store faster than 1 full payment.

7 STEPS TO HAVING "BEAST CREDIT SCORE" -THE QUICK AND DIRTY

(1) You should have your credit report but if not then order it. Face the music. You need to know what your current status is. Period. Order your credit report online or via mail. I say print it out because you should write on the reports. Another option is to sign up for www.myfico.com to see your actual credit score which you need to know at the beginning of this process; there is a small fee involved but well worth it because when anything changes on your report the agency will alert you via text and/or email. Another service is www.creditkarma.com it is free but the numbers are not accurate; usually credit karma score is 20-30 below what your actual score is and updating is slower than other services.

(2) Create yourself a "War Room" in your house. It can be a section in your shoe room or in your

Man Cave. Just create a space to monitor and tackle your credit. A place where you track and post your credit progress. This is a long term part time job. Have this room out from the flow of the house. Put your reports on the wall if you to just to see where you been, where you are and where you want to go. I also believe that you should create a targeted Vision Board. It is a myth that you need to begin it at the beginning of the year. You need to create it when the idea enters your mind and update if necessary once you believe you are finished. With this financial and credit report Vision Board, be as specific as you can. The universe hears you. Put on that board pay off $50,000 of students. Pay back parents $10,000 that you owe them. Pay vehicle #1 off by end of the year with second income monies.

(3) Once reports arrive make 1 to 2 copies and keep an original in a separate file in your filing system. Keep one that you do not write on because you will be tracking the corrections.

(4) Diligence and Persistence is your next critical step. Do not give up. When tired of fighting take a 2 day break and get back to fighting the creditors and the agency. It is ok to be polite on the phone when you talk to creditor or agency. Your priority is increasing your credit score not making enemies. Stay positive in the process.

Go through every single line on your credit reports. As previously stated look for errors and inconsistencies. From your name or names, address to balances and account numbers. Think like a creditor, would you feel

comfortable lending money to someone that has a new address every year like a transient. Have all addresses removed except your momma house and where you live at now. Do the same with misspelled versions of your name, have them corrected or removed from your credit report. You want to appear consistent and responsible. If you separated from spouse go ahead and divorce them too before they get in debt while still legally married and creditor seeks payment from legal spouse. GET A FRESH START ON IT ALL!

Locate any errors on credit report, circle and number them on the actual report. Once completed refer to the corresponding numbers when you are writing your dispute letter refer to their credit report. You

CREDIT REPORT

- JANE DOE
  1234 FIRST STREET
  CALABASSAS, CA 90a90

ITEM 1 — Nelnet

Credit Acceptance

ITEM 2 — Board of Water and Lights

Consumer Energy

Wells Fargo

Cadillac Financial

Macys Credit Card

ITEM 3 — USAA Credit union

September 2018

want to appear organized right out the gate so the agency know you are serious and will not be going giving up or going away. As you are circling errors have a laptop nearby and type your letter out right then indicating that the item is invalid, incorrect or invalid, so must be DELETED.

Next go through all balances and if the amount is incorrect in any part, deny the balance completely. It Is either 100% right or it is wrong. Make the credit agency and creditor validate and verify the debt if they cannot validate, then request DELETION.

If you any collections accounts are listed request validation of the debt from the original creditor (there is a sample of this at the end of this book). They might not have the original contract if it is with a Collection Agency. Deny and request immediate deletion within 30 days.

ALL inquires deny and request validation within 30 days. Inquiry only have small effect on credit score but you need every single point, so if any inquiry is not yours, request immediate deletion.

(5) Wait for the Mail. I will not guarantee it but if you check your credit score after all of the inaccuracies your score will go up 10-25 points. That is huge difference if you trying to get over the 575 or 600 hump to finance a car or get an apartment.

(6) After that is done. Start negotiating with remaining collection accounts if any and get those settled and deleted.

(7) Then contact THE CREDIT BEAST, INC. At www.creditbeastinc.com to boost up your score QUICK. Your credit is nothing to gamble with. Contact www.creditbeastinc.com and

within 40-60 days increase your credit score by using the strategies of Credit Beast Boosting System. Boost meaning depending on package it could go up 100 points, that would put you in entirely different credit and interest bracket.

MY CREDIT SMART NOTES #6

TRUTH #7 If All Else Fails You Have Last Resort Option

When building your credit to get into the BLACK. The goal is to eliminate all negative marks from your credit. However if the debt is overwhelming and causing stress you do have a last resort option, BANKRUPTCY

"The wicked borrows and does not pay back, but the righteous is gracious and gives". - Psalm 37:21

BANKRUPTCY INFORMATION SHEET

BANKRUPTCY LAW IS A FEDERAL LAW. THIS SHEET PROVIDES YOU WITH GENERAL INFORMATION ABOUT WHAT HAPPENS IN A BANKRUPTCY CASE. THE INFORMATION HERE IS NOT COMPLETE. YOU MAY NEED LEGAL ADVICE.

<u>WHEN YOU FILE BANKRUPTCY</u>

You can choose the kind of bankruptcy that best meets your needs (provided you meet certain qualifications):

Chapter 7 – A trustee is appointed to take over your property. Any property of value will be sold or turned into money to pay your creditors. You may be able to keep some personal items and possibly real estate depending on the law of the State where you live and applicable federal laws.

Chapter 13 – You can usually keep your property, but you must earn wages or have some other source of regular income and you must agree to pay part of your income to your creditors. The court must approve your repayment plan and your budget. A trustee is appointed and will collect the payments from you, pay your creditors, and make sure you live up to the terms of your repayment plan.

Chapter 12 – Like chapter 13, but it is only for family farmers and family fishermen.

Chapter 11 – This is used mostly by businesses. In chapter 11, you may continue to operate your business, but your creditors and the court must approve a plan to repay your debts. There is no trustee unless the judge decides that one is necessary; if a trustee is appointed, the trustee takes control of your business and property.

If you have already filed bankruptcy under chapter 7, you may be able to change your case to another chapter.

Your bankruptcy may be reported on your credit record for as long as ten years. It can affect your ability to receive credit in the future.

WHAT IS A BANKRUPTCY DISCHARGE AND HOW DOES IT OPERATE?

One of the reasons people file bankruptcy is to get a "discharge." A discharge is a court order which states that you do not have to pay most of your debts. Some debts cannot be discharged. For example, you cannot discharge debts for–

- most taxes;
- child support;
- alimony;
- most student loans;

- court fines and criminal restitution; and
- personal injury caused by driving drunk or under the influence of drugs.

The discharge only applies to debts that arose before the date you filed. Also, if the judge finds that you received money or property by fraud, that debt may not be discharged.

It is important to list all your property and debts in your bankruptcy schedules. If you do not list a debt, for example, it is possible the debt will not be discharged. The judge can also deny your discharge if you do something dishonest in connection with your bankruptcy case, such as destroy or hide property, falsify records, or lie, or if you disobey a court order.

You can only receive a chapter 7 discharge once every eight years. Other rules may apply if you previously received a discharge in a chapter 13 case. No one can make you pay a debt that has been discharged, but you can voluntarily pay any debt you wish to pay. You do not have to sign a reaffirmation agreement (see below) or any other kind of document to do this.

Some creditors hold a secured claim (for example, the bank that holds the mortgage on your house or the loan company that has a lien on your car). You do not have to pay a secured claim if the debt is discharged, but the creditor can still take the property.

WHAT IS A REAFFIRMATION AGREEMENT?

Even if a debt can be discharged, you may have special reasons why you want to promise to pay it. For example, you may want to work out a plan with the bank to keep your car. To promise to pay that debt, you must sign and file a reaffirmation agreement with the court. Reaffirmation agreements are under special rules and are voluntary. They are not required by bankruptcy law or by any other law. Reaffirmation agreements–

- must be voluntary;
- must not place too heavy a burden on you or your family;
- must be in your best interest; and
- can be cancelled anytime before the court issues your discharge or within 60 days after the agreement is filed with the court, whichever gives you the most time.

If you are an individual and you are not represented by an attorney, the court must hold a hearing to decide whether to approve the reaffirmation agreement. The agreement will not be legally binding until the court approves it.

If you reaffirm a debt and then fail to pay it, you owe the debt the same as though there was no bankruptcy. The debt will not be discharged and the creditor can take action to recover any property on which it has a lien or mortgage. The creditor can also take legal action to recover a judgment against you.

IF YOU WANT MORE INFORMATION OR HAVE ANY QUESTIONS ABOUT HOW THE BANKRUPTCY LAWS AFFECT YOU, YOU MAY NEED LEGAL ADVICE. THE TRUSTEE IN YOUR CASE IS NOT RESPONSIBLE FORGIVING YOU LEGAL ADVICE.

STEP 7 – Last Resort: Bankruptcy

Bankruptcy is a tool with a high price to pay when the bills and stress of the bills are weighing on you. Keep this as a last resort option. If you can see any other method use it and avoid filing bankruptcy at all cost. The only people that win are the lawyers and the system. The average price of filing for bankruptcy is $700-$4000 depending on which type you file. AVOID.

Know that there are 2 different types of consumer bankruptcies (a) Chapter 13 which is a reorganization. In this process the federal court and Trustee have control over how your spend your money for the next 3-5 years all while paying themselves thousands of dollars. At the end of this process some creditors will get no money while others obtain a small % of what was owed. In this process your credit score can increase because creditors are receiving some monies

(b) A Chapter 7 bankruptcy is a liquidation shorter process. Your credit score is not increasing as a matter of fact as soon as you are assigned a case number it is almost guaranteed that your score will drop by 100 points. However in 3-6 months when this process is completely over you will owe no one; maybe secured creditors like your car you are keeping. Your Attorney fees are due 1 time; not multiple times over a 3-5 year period. Once you receive your discharge contact www.creditbeastinc.com for a Credit Boost program.

Here Are a Few Tips to Avoid Filing Bankruptcy: KEEP a job, any type of job. There is no hope of managing your debt if you have no income. You are delusional if you think you can manage debt with no money. This is not the time to follow a dream and start a business as your only income. If you have a dream you are pursuing, pursue it on the side and keep steady income too. I HAVE A DREAM motto is fine, but live in reality right now. NOW your reality is paying down bills. **TIP**: Increasing your personal credit score high will allow you to be the guarantor on your future business loan. So do not jump up and quit your job because everyone is doing their own business on INSTAGRAM. Until your business flourishes KEEP YOUR PAY CHECK.

For now:

> (1) STOP SPENDING. Since you have a steady job you got to eat lunch while at work. Cook your food for lunch daily. Yes it is cumbersome but you are trying to get out of the RED and get in the BLACK to have better credit and more money to enjoy your life. The time will come again when you can go to the *Cheesecake Factory* and *London Chop House*. That prepping technique used for weight management you can also use for money management as well. Prepare to save in advance. Incorporate kids and spouse in this new saving system. Buy your beverages at ALDI or dollar store and take to work. Do not hit the vending machine for no reason. You are no longer in the business of

making others money, you are creating money for self to pay down your creditors.

(2) THIS MAY NOT BE A GOOD TIME TO SAVE EITHER. Of course pay tithes maybe not offerings (you got to deal with religion on your own). Take offering and pay down a bill weekly even if it is just $35 a week. One medical bill for $100 can be paid off in 3 small payments then next month resume offering, I think God or whomever you worship will understand.

(3) If overtime is available at job, get all of it that you can get work it moderately and use extra to pay down bills, not to vacation or splurge on beauty maintenance. This is the time to learn how to cut your own hair or go to beauty

school and pay a nominal fee. Also until you get on the right financial track this may not be the time to continue with nail maintenance, a simple at home manicure is cheaper. Products $5.00 and to pay for service is $35 bi-weekly. That difference of $30 can be paid on a bill. Remember this is only temporary you will be back fabulous and living within your means in no time.

(4) If possible abandon driving car to work totally, catch public transportation this cuts stress, gas cost and lessons the untimely possibility of car repairs. Car repairs will drive a sane person insane, especially when you trying so hard to get on track and manage your money. The last thing you want is a big car repair expense. Buy a bus pass for work and bus/train it for 1-3 months it will change your financial life!

I remember when my first bankruptcy client came into my office. I thought to myself why hasn't he paid his bills, this client had been working the same job for over 15 years, previously married and paid no one. I thought how irresponsible, then he explained that he was overwhelmed by his divorce, trying to be a single parent and could not even manage himself let alone 24 pages of debt including wife medical bills.

I also remember the last clients I took. They were the clients from HELL, not living at all in reality. Blaming the world for their finances, I will go back to the same original concept. KEEP A JOB/INCOME (A Steady Eddie).

The bills are more than likely manageable with some money. It was so much wrong with this financially dysfunctional client life. It is a commercial that says when your spouse has an addiction, the family has an addiction. In this case the husband was an uncontrollable alcoholic, but working and the wife was a delusional woman who had left a job under fraudulent pretences. She desperately wanted to be a housewife to a 16 year old child while receiving child support from a previous relationship with married a man.

ALL bad signs and addictions: alcohol addiction and lying addiction, which destroyed the financial stability of the household.

RESULT: They could not pay their bills because the creditors call to much and it was too much stress. The truth of the matter is the wife wanted to be a Housewife of Atlanta, but she needed to get a job, keep it and quit thinking she is married to Donald Trump instead of Jim Chump. Work a job and pay your way out of the debt is the best answer. Subsequently the bankruptcy failed because they were reorganizing and needed more money to pay their secured creditors, mainly expensive cars they could not afford.

Quit blaming others and manage your bills before filing bankruptcy. Chances are it will fail and/or you will have to file again because it is your bad habits and lack of living within your means that is the problem.

Do not worry about the creditor calls. A creditor can only call 2-3 times per week and between the hours of 8am-9pm any other communication is prohibited. The 4 principals of Telephone Consumer Protection Act of 1991 says: (1) proper calls identification requirements must be met (2) calling hours restriction (3) if customer says do not call it must cease and desist and (4) adherence to auto dialler and automatic dialling recorded message (ADRMP) regulation must be followed. Once you file bankruptcy and receive a file case number all collections calls must stop. IT IS THE LAW!

AFTER BANKRUPTCY- NOW WHAT?

Oh goodness your bankruptcy is complete!!! What do you do next? First take a breathier and be happy that the trustee didn't take the shirt off your back. In Michigan which you would think is a debtor friendly state, it is actually a creditor state and in the highest unemployed recessed state in the country the Trustees are forcing people to sell property to payback some creditors. I am hoping that you are not in that category. Now you have no creditors and guess what you have no credit. This means you have peace, but now need to rebuild your credit and reprioritize your life.

With this new fresh start manage the bills and do not let them manage you. Do not create new unnecessary bills.

I am sure before you received those bankruptcy discharge papers creditors were sending you new pre-approvals to obtain a new vehicle and new credit cards. Pause-do not mail them back. After bankruptcy you more than likely owe no one except those secured creditors that you decided to retain (For example: your car or house).

Obtaining new credit is important but this time you got to be careful. Before you obtain new credit cards and start spending again which will end you back in debt. FIGURE OUT HOW TO KEEP THE MONEY THAT YOU HAVE IN YOUR POCKET FIRST!

It appears that now you have extra money and can do what you want. Well, you cannot. Stop acting as if you are allergic to money, stop letting it go out the door this time be frugal and smart. Start reading this book from the beginning and employ these principles I have laid out. THEN read again.

MY CREDIT SMART NOTES #7

CHANGE YOUR HABITS.

CHANGE YOUR LIFE.

YOU DESERVE ALL THE CREDIT.

CHECKLIST

- ✔ Look @ check stub net pay
- ✔ List all necessary bills
- ✔ Do the real math, do not guess
- ✔ If in positive go to * on list, if not next checkmark
- ✔ You are in negative you must generate more income. Seize all luxury spending for example: Netflix subscription, gel nails, bath & body works and Happy Hour with friends
- ✔ *take ½ of extra money and put in emergency fund account
- ✔ Get credit report
- ✔ Order myfico.com
- ✔ Take other half of leftover money and pay an old bill, minimally make a payment
- ✔ Repeat until all bills are paid off
- ✔ Clear up credit report inaccuracies
- ✔ NOW contact www.creditbeastinc.com to use Boosting System
- ✔

SOURCE LIST

U.S. Bankruptcy Court

Brainy Quotes, (2018)

Random Quote Generator, (2018)

Fair Debt Collection Practices Act

(FDCPA) of 1977

www.unsplash.com

https://www.statista.com/topics/1156/coupon-market-trends-in-the-united-states/

https://www.usatoday.com/story/money/personalfinance/retirement/2018/07/22/could-you-get-by-on-average-retirement-income/36848957/

ROADMAP TO FINANCIAL AND CREDIT FREEDOM

TAX REFUND CHECKLIST

- ✔ Get Exact Number from Tax Preparer.
- ✔ While you wait, plan and research.
- ✔ Plan spending before you obtain return down to the penny.
- ✔ Write down what you need. For example: catch up on light bill or taxes.
- ✔ Write the plan down not just random. Before you know it, the money will be gone.
- ✔ Once you receive money hold onto it for 24 hours to avoid fake emergencies or impulse shopping.
- ✔ Shopping spree is not a need.
- ✔ If you plan to start a business after catching up on bills, START

IT NOW NO MATTER WHAT.
Contact 24karatkollectionllc@gmail.com for beauty vendor list and mentoring. They handle not just hair but all beauty contacts. 24/7 ebook available and mentor services.

- ✅ If you are investing in you are interested in profile credit updating contact and dispute letters 24karatkollectionllc@gmail.com for package prices and timelines.
- ✅ If you goal is to improve your credit life go to www.creditbeastinc.com for credit boost.
- ✅ Do not get distracted with fantasy rich life; this only happens once a year. Make

good decisions so that you will have a good rest of the year.

TAX REFUND PLAN SHEET

Step 1: Get Sign Up for Credit Boost Program. www.creditbeastinc.com

Step 2:

Step 3:

Step 4:

Step 5:

Step 6:

Step 7:

Step 8:

Step 9:

Step 10:

SAMPLE Request for VALIDATION- NOT Verification

Your Name
Your Street Address
Your City, State and Zip Code

August 29th, 2019

 Company: NCO FINANCIAL SYSTEMS INC.

Address:

City/ State/ Zip:

RE: Account # 000

To Whom It May Concern:

This letter is being sent to you in response to notices sent to me from your company and more importantly, due to your erroneous reporting to the Credit Bureau{s}, the highly negative impact on my personal credit report. Please be advised that this is not a refusal to pay, but a notice sent pursuant to the Fair Debt Collection Practices Act, 15 USC 1692g Sec. 809 {b} that your claim is disputed and validation is requested.

This is NOT a request for "verification" or proof of my mailing address, but a request for VALIDATION made pursuant to the above named Title and Section. I respectfully request that your offices provide me with competent evidence that I have any legal obligation to pay you.

Please provide me with the following:

- What the money you say I owe is for:
- Explain and show me how you calculated what you say I owe:
- Provide me with copies of any papers that show I agreed to pay what you say I owe:
- Provide a verification or copy of any judgment if applicable:
- Identify the original creditor:
- Prove the Statute of Limitations has not expired on this account:
- Show me the you are licensed to collect in my state:
- Provide me with your license numbers and Registered Agent or Agent of Service:

At this time I will also inform you that if your offices have reported invalidated information to any of the 3 major Credit Bureau's {Experian, Equifax or TransUnion} this action might constitute fraud under both Federal and State Laws. Due to this fact, if any negative mark is found on any of my credit reports by your company or the company that you represent, I will not hesitate to bring legal action against you for the following:

- Violation of the Fair Credit Reporting Act
- Violation of the Fair Debt Collection Practices Act
- Defamation of Character

If your offices are able to provide proper documentation as requested in the following Declaration, I will require at least 30 days to investigate this information and during such time all collection activity must cease and desist.

Also, during this validation period, if any action is taken which could be considered detrimental to any of my credit reports, I will consult with my legal counsel for suit. This includes listing any information with a credit reporting repository that could be inaccurate or invalidated or verifying an account as accurate, when it fact there is no provided proof that it is accurate.

If your company fails to respond to this validation request within 30 days from the date of your receipt, all references to this account must be deleted and completely removed from my credit report and a copy of such deletion {to any/all of the 3 major credit reporting bureaus: Equifax, Experian and TransUnion} request shall be sent to me immediately.

I would also like to request, in writing, that no telephone contact be made by your company to my home or my place of employment. If your offices attempt telephone communication with me, including but not limited to computer generated calls and calls or correspondence sent to or with any third parties, it will be considered harassment and I will have no choice but to file suit. All future communications with me MUST be done in writing and sent to the address noted in this letter by USPS.

It would be advisable that you assure your records are in order before I am forced to take legal action against your company and your client. This is an attempt to correct your records; any information obtained shall be used for that purpose.

Best Regards,

Your Name

SAMPLE: Intent To file Lawsuit- No Response For Validation Documentation

September 16, 2019

Equifax Information Services LLC

RE: Intent to file lawsuit-no response for Validation documentation

Validation Letter sent to: American Express

Account #0000

To Whom It May Concern:

With this letter I am informing you that I requested "validation" {not verification} of an item reported to you by the above original creditor/collection agency. I have received no response from them and/or no proof to validate their claim.

They have broken the law by their non response within the time period allowed by law. I am proceeding with legal action as prescribed by law against the above named original creditor/collection agency. Should this item not be deleted within the required time allowed by law I will seek every legal remedy available to me and file suit against the credit bureau responsible for reporting this erroneous claim.

I urge you to take this extremely serious as I have documented my case without error. I encourage a response from you expeditiously.

Sincerely

Your Name

52 WEEK MONEY CHALLENGE

WEEK	DEPOSIT AMOUNT	ACCOUNT BALANCE	WEEK	DEPOSIT AMOUNT	ACCOUNT BALANCE
1	$1.00	$1.00	27	$27.00	$378.00
2	$2.00	$3.00	28	$28.00	$406.00
3	$3.00	$6.00	29	$29.00	$435.00
4	$4.00	$10.00	30	$30.00	$465.00
5	$5.00	$15.00	31	$31.00	$496.00
6	$6.00	$21.00	32	$32.00	$528.00
7	$7.00	$28.00	33	$33.00	$561.00
8	$8.00	$36.00	34	$34.00	$595.00
9	$9.00	$45.00	35	$35.00	$630.00
10	$10.00	$55.00	36	$36.00	$666.00
11	$11.00	$66.00	37	$37.00	$703.00
12	$12.00	$78.00	38	$38.00	$741.00
13	$13.00	$91.00	39	$39.00	$780.00
14	$14.00	$105.00	40	$40.00	$820.00
15	$15.00	$120.00	41	$41.00	$861.00
16	$16.00	$136.00	42	$42.00	$903.00
17	$17.00	$153.00	43	$43.00	$946.00
18	$18.00	$171.00	44	$44.00	$990.00
19	$19.00	$190.00	45	$45.00	$1035.00
20	$20.00	$210.00	46	$46.00	$1081.00
21	$21.00	$231.00	47	$47.00	$1128.00
22	$22.00	$253.00	48	$48.00	$1176.00
23	$23.00	$276.00	49	$49.00	$1225.00
24	$24.00	$300.00	50	$50.00	$1275.00
25	$25.00	$325.00	51	$51.00	$1326.00
26	$26.00	$351.00	52	$52.00	$1378.00

CREDIT REPORT DISPUTE SHEET

Creditor #1 _____

Dispute _____

Date Mailed _____

Solution Requested _____

Due Date Rt. _____

Creditor #2 _____

Dispute _____

Date Mailed _____

Solution Requested _____

Due Date Rt. _____

CREDIT REPORT DISPUTE SHEET

Creditor #3 _____

Dispute _____

Date Mailed _____

Solution Requested _____

Due Date Rt. _____

Creditor #4 _____

Dispute _____

Date Mailed _____

Solution Requested _____

Due Date Rt. _____

CREDIT REPORT DISPUTE SHEET

Creditor #5 _____

Dispute _____

Date Mailed _____

Solution Requested _____

Due Date Rt. _____

Creditor #6 _____

Dispute _____

Date Mailed _____

Solution Requested _____

Due Date Rt. _____

CREDIT REPORT DISPUTE SHEET

Creditor #7 _____

Dispute _____

Date Mailed _____

Solution Requested _____

Due Date Rt. _____

Creditor #8 _____

Dispute _____

Date Mailed _____

Solution Requested _____

Due Date Rt. _____

CREDIT REPORT DISPUTE SHEET

Creditor #9 _____

Dispute _____

Date Mailed _____

Solution Requested _____

Due Date Rt. _____

Creditor #10 _____

Dispute _____

Date Mailed _____

Solution Requested _____

Due Date Rt. _____

www.ingramcontent.com/pod-product-compliance
Lightning Source LLC
Chambersburg PA
CBHW042313150426
43200CB00001B/9